HOW TO BECOME A MILLIONAIRE
WITHOUT TRADING TIME FOR MONEY

BREAKING THE SHACKLES OF
FINANCIAL LIMITATION

GREAT ALEEM

2

COPYRIGHT

TABLE OF CONTENTS

INTRODUCTION

Welcome to "Millionaire Mindset," a comprehensive guide that will transform your financial journey and liberate you from the shackles of the 9 to 5 drama. In this book, we'll explore the principles, strategies, and mindset shifts required to pave your way to financial abundance and break free from the conventional work grind.

DEFINING YOUR FINANCIAL VISION

What does wealth mean to you

In the quaint town of Crestwood, John, a software engineer, and Muhammed, an aspiring entrepreneur, found themselves caught in the relentless rhythm of the 9-to-5 grind. Both shared a common dream: to break free from the conventional work drama and achieve financial prosperity. One day, over a cup of coffee at their favorite local café, they decided it was time to redefine their paths and pursue a life of abundance.

John and Muhammed began their journey by defining their visions for wealth. Each took a moment to close their eyes and imagine a life where financial stress was replaced by security and freedom. John envisioned a life where his software skills were not just a means of earning a paycheck but a tool to create innovative solutions that impacted lives globally. Muhammed, on the other hand, saw himself at the helm of a thriving business, one that not only brought financial success but also contributed to the well-being of his community.

As they clarified their financial goals, John and Muhammed realized the importance of specificity. No longer satisfied with vague aspirations, they outlined their dreams with vivid detail. John set a goal to launch a tech startup within the next three years, providing a tangible timeline to his vision. Muhammed, fueled by his passion for sustainability, outlined plans for an eco-friendly business that aligned with his values.

Their visions were not limited to personal gain; both John and Muhammed aspired to be pillars of support for their communities. John imagined a company that not only created jobs but also invested in education and mentorship programs. Muhammed envisioned his business as a force for positive change, implementing environmentally conscious practices and contributing to local charities.

With their visions firmly in place, John and Muhammed felt a renewed sense of purpose. They recognized that the journey toward wealth was a marathon, not a sprint, and each financial goal was a crucial mile marker on their path.

John's first goal was to leverage his programming skills to create a side hustle. He started developing software solutions for small businesses, gradually building a client base. Muhammed, with a background in sustainable practices, began researching and planning his eco-friendly business model.

As they achieved their initial goals, John and Muhammed delved into the realm of investments. They educated themselves on stocks, real estate, and other wealth-building avenues. Recognizing that wealth creation often involved taking calculated risks, they embraced the learning curve with determination.

With each milestone, John and Muhammed celebrated not only their financial successes but also the personal growth that accompanied their journey. The once-dull routine of their lives transformed into a vibrant tapestry of experiences, each contributing to their overall sense of accomplishment.

Their story teaches us that defining a vision for wealth and clarifying financial goals isn't just a strategic exercise; it's a transformative journey. It's about understanding that wealth goes beyond personal gain; it's about crafting a life that aligns with one's deepest desires and contributes positively to the world. As the sun set on Crestwood, John and Muhammed stood on the cusp of their dreams, a testament to the power of defining one's vision and pursuing it with unwavering determination.

CLARIFYING YOUR JOURNEY TOWARDS
FINANCIAL FREEDOM

In the quaint town of Crestwood, John, a software engineer, and Muhammed, an aspiring entrepreneur, found themselves caught in the relentless rhythm of the 9-to-5 grind. Both shared a common dream: to break free from the conventional work drama and achieve financial prosperity. One day, over a cup of coffee at their favorite local café, they decided it was time to redefine their paths and pursue a life of abundance.

John and Muhammed began their journey by defining their visions for wealth. Each took a moment to close their eyes and imagine a life where financial stress was replaced by security and freedom. John envisioned a life where his software skills were not just a means of earning a paycheck but a tool to create innovative solutions that impacted lives globally. Muhammed, on the other hand, saw himself at the helm of a thriving business, one that not only brought financial success but also contributed to the well-being of his community. As they clarified their financial goals, John and Muhammed realized the importance of specificity. No longer satisfied with vague aspirations, they outlined their dreams with vivid detail. John set a goal to launch a tech startup within the next three years, providing a tangible timeline to his vision. Muhammed, fueled by his passion for sustainability, outlined plans for an eco-friendly business that aligned with his values.

Their visions were not limited to personal gain; both John and Muhammed aspired to be pillars of support for their communities. John imagined a company that not only created jobs but also invested in education and mentorship programs. Muhammed envisioned his business as a force for positive change, implementing environmentally conscious practices and contributing to local charities.

With their visions firmly in place, John and Muhammed felt a renewed sense of purpose. They recognized that the journey toward wealth was a marathon, not a sprint, and each financial goal was a crucial mile marker on their path.

John's first goal was to leverage his programming skills to create a side hustle. He started developing software solutions for small businesses, gradually building a client base. Muhammed, with a background in sustainable practices, began researching and planning his eco-friendly business model.

As they achieved their initial goals, John and Muhammed delved into the realm of investments. They educated themselves on stocks, real estate, and other wealth-building avenues. Recognizing that wealth creation often involved taking calculated risks, they embraced the learning curve with determination.

With each milestone, John and Muhammed celebrated not only their financial successes but also the personal growth that accompanied their journey. The once-dull routine of their lives transformed into a vibrant tapestry of experiences, each contributing to their overall sense of accomplishment.

Their story teaches us that defining a vision for wealth and clarifying financial goals isn't just a strategic exercise; it's a transformative journey. It's about understanding that wealth goes beyond personal gain; it's about crafting a life that aligns with one's deepest desires and contributes positively to the world. As the sun set on Crestwood, John and Muhammed stood on the cusp of their dreams, a testament to the power of defining one's vision and pursuing it with unwavering determination.

Master your financial mindset

John and Muhammed's mastery of their financial mindsets was a gradual process, marked by deliberate actions, mindset shifts, and a commitment to continuous learning. Here's how they approached mastering their financial mindsets

CULTIVATING A POSITIVE MINDSET

• John: Actively practiced gratitude and positive affirmations. Focused on the opportunities within challenges and visualized the success of his endeavors.

• Muhammed: Embraced a mindset of abundance, acknowledging that there were ample opportunities for success. Adopted positive self-talk to overcome doubts and setbacks.

Overcoming Limiting Beliefs

• John: Identified and challenged his limiting beliefs about entrepreneurship and risk. Actively sought out success stories of entrepreneurs who overcame similar challenges.

• Muhammed: Acknowledged and confronted doubts about the viability of eco-friendly business models. Surrounding himself with mentors who had successfully implemented sustainable practices helped him overcome skepticism.

Embracing a Growth Mindset John saw obstacles as chances to improve and expand.

Regularly sought feedback and constructive criticism to improve both himself and his business.

• Muhammed: Considered setbacks as temporary obstacles on the path to success. Embraced the idea that learning and improvement were ongoing processes.

Building Multiple Income Streams

• John: Leveraged his programming skills to create a side hustle, generating additional income. Diversified his investments in stocks and explored real estate opportunities.

• Muhammed: Turned his passion for sustainability into a business, creating a diversified income stream. Explored partnerships and collaborations to enhance revenue streams.

Entrepreneurial Pursuits

• John: Actively sought out entrepreneurial opportunities within his field of expertise, eventually launching a tech startup. Embraced calculated risks and learned from failures.

• Muhammed: Transformed his passion for sustainability into a viable business model. Navigated the challenges of entrepreneurship with resilience, adapting his strategies when necessary.

Financial Literacy:

• John: Invested time in understanding the intricacies of the stock market, real estate, and financial planning. Regularly read books and attended workshops to stay informed.

• Muhammed: Combined his passion for sustainability with financial acumen, ensuring that his business decisions aligned with both ethical and profitable outcomes.

7. Networking and Relationship Building:

• John: Actively participated in industry events, built a professional network, and sought mentorship from experienced entrepreneurs. imparted to others his wisdom and experiences

• Muhammed: Formed partnerships within the sustainability community, attended conferences, and engaged in mentorship relationships. Recognized the value of a supportive network.

8. Embracing Failure and Learning from Setbacks:

• John: Viewed failures as opportunities to iterate and improve his business model. Learned from each setback and adjusted his strategies accordingly.

• Muhammed: Accepted failures as part of the entrepreneurial journey. Used setbacks as learning experiences, refining his approach to overcome challenges.

LIFESTYLE DESIGN:

• John: Balanced work and personal life, ensuring that success didn't come at the expense of well-being. Incorporated travel and experiences into his lifestyle.

• Muhammed: Designed his business to align with his values and desired lifestyle. Prioritized a balanced life that allowed for personal fulfillment and professional success.

Through these deliberate actions and mindset shifts, John and Muhammed not only mastered their financial mindsets but also cultivated a holistic approach to wealth that went beyond mere accumulation.

Their commitment to continuous learning, resilience in the face of challenges, and a positive outlook were key elements in their journey toward financial mastery and a life of abundance.

Building multiple income streams

John and Muhammed strategically built multiple income streams by leveraging their skills, passions, and entrepreneurial spirit. Here's a closer look at how each of them diversified their sources of income:

John's Approach:

1. Side Hustle in Software Development:

• Utilizing Skills: John recognized the demand for his programming skills beyond his full-time job. He started a side hustle, offering software development services to small businesses.

• Online Presence: Established an online presence through a professional website and social media platforms to attract clients interested in his expertise.

2. Investing in Stocks:

• Financial Literacy: Dedicated time to understand the stock market and investment strategies.

• Diversification: Spread his investments across a diverse portfolio, minimizing risks and maximizing potential returns.

3. Real Estate Ventures:

• Educating Himself: Took the time to learn about real estate, attending workshops, and seeking advice from experienced investors.

• Strategic Investments: Identified and invested in real estate opportunities that aligned with his financial goals, such as rental properties or real estate crowdfunding.

Muhammed's Approach:

Eco-Friendly Business:

• Passion to Profit: Transformed his passion for sustainability into a business. Developed eco-friendly products or services that resonated with consumers.

• Market Research: Conducted thorough market research to identify gaps and needs within the sustainable products market.

Partnerships and Collaborations

:

• Building Relationships: Actively sought partnerships with other businesses that shared his values. Collaborated on joint ventures or co-branded initiatives.

• Expanding Reach: Leveraged partnerships to expand the reach of his products and services, tapping into new customer bases.

Investing in Renewable Energy:

• Aligned Investments: Invested in renewable energy projects or companies that aligned with his commitment to sustainability.

• Combining Values and Finance: Ensured that his investment choices reflected not only financial considerations but also environmental and social values.

Consulting and Workshops:

• Sharing Expertise: Recognized his expertise in sustainability and offered consulting services to businesses looking to adopt eco-friendly practices.

• Educational Workshops: Conducted workshops on sustainable living and business practices, generating additional income while spreading awareness

COMMON STRATEGIES

Continuous Learning:

• Financial Education: Both John and Muhammed prioritized continuous learning. They stayed informed about new investment opportunities, market trends, and business strategies.

2 Networking Building Connections: Actively networked within their industries. Networking not only led to new opportunities but also provided insights and support from like-minded individuals.

• Balancing Risk and Reward:

3 Calculated Risks: While embracing the entrepreneurial spirit, both John and Muhammed took calculated risks. They carefully evaluated each opportunity to ensure alignment with their goals.

• Adaptability:

4 Flexibility: Acknowledging that markets and trends change, both entrepreneurs remained adaptable. They adjusted their strategies based on evolving circumstances.

By combining their skills, passions, and strategic thinking, John and Muhammed created a diversified portfolio of income streams. This approach not only increased their financial resilience but also allowed them to explore different facets of their interests and contribute to their overall sense of fulfillment and success.

More tips on income generation

SCALING AND AUTOMATING:

1. Tech Startup Expansion (John):

• Scaling Operations: As John's tech startup gained traction, he focused on scaling operations. This involved hiring skilled professionals, expanding product offerings, and reaching new markets.

• Automation: Implemented automation tools and systems to streamline processes, freeing up time for strategic decision-making and exploring additional ventures.

2. Eco-Friendly Product Lines (Muhammed):

• Product Diversification: Muhammed expanded his eco-friendly business by diversifying product lines. This not only attracted a broader customer base but also mitigated risks associated with market fluctuations.

• Supply Chain Optimization: Automated certain aspects of the supply chain to enhance efficiency and reduce operational costs.

Passive Income Streams:

1. Investment Portfolios (Both):

• Dividend Stocks: Both John and Muhammed included dividend-paying stocks in their portfolios, generating a steady stream of passive income.

• Real Estate Rental Income: Income from rental properties became a reliable source of passive cash flow, offering financial stability.

2. Monetizing Expertise (John and Muhammed):

• Online Courses and Consultations: Recognizing their expertise, both entrepreneurs created online courses and offered consulting services. This provided an additional income stream with relatively low ongoing effort.

Giving Back and Monetizing Passion:

Philanthropy Initiatives

• Corporate Social Responsibility: Incorporated philanthropy into their businesses. Portions of profits were allocated to charitable causes, aligning their financial success with social responsibility.

• Positive Impact: The positive social impact of their businesses not only contributed to a sense of purpose but also enhanced brand reputation, attracting socially conscious consumers.

Educational Platforms

• Blogging and Podcasting: Both John and Muhammed started blogs and podcasts related to their industries. These platforms generated income through sponsorships, advertising, and affiliate marketing while sharing valuable insights.

Exit Strategies and Portfolio Management:

1. Strategic Exits (John):

• Selling Successful Ventures: If an opportunity presented itself, John considered strategic exits from certain ventures, capitalizing on their success to fund new initiatives.

• Portfolio Rebalancing: Regularly assessed his investment portfolio, adjusting holdings to align with changing market conditions and personal financial goals.

2. Diversification (Muhammed):

• Continued Diversification: Muhammed maintained a commitment to diversification, periodically reassessing his business ventures and investments to ensure a well-balanced and resilient portfolio.

Reflecting on the Journey

1. Personal Growth and Fulfillment (Both):

• Celebrating Milestones: Regularly celebrated milestones, acknowledging not only financial achievements but personal growth throughout the journey.

• Work-Life Harmony: Strived to maintain a healthy work-life balance, recognizing that financial success should contribute to overall well-being and fulfillment.

2. Mentoring Others (Both):

• Paying It Forward: Actively engaged in mentoring aspiring entrepreneurs, sharing their experiences and knowledge to empower others on their financial journeys.

• Community Impact: The impact of their mentorship extended beyond individual success, contributing to the growth and resilience of their local entrepreneurial communities.

John and Muhammed's ability to build and sustain multiple income streams was rooted in a combination of strategic decision-making, adaptability, and a commitment to continuous learning. As they continued to navigate the dynamic landscape of entrepreneurship and investments, their diversified approach not only enhanced their financial well-being but also allowed them to contribute positively to their communities and industries. The journey toward financial mastery was not just about accumulating wealth; it was a holistic pursuit of a meaningful and balanced life.

John's Entrepreneurial Pursuit Plan

1. Tech Startup Launch:

• Objective: Launch a tech startup within three years.

• Strategies:

• Market Research: Identify unmet needs and trends in the tech industry.

• Networking: Build connections with potential collaborators, mentors, and investors.

• Prototyping: Develop and test prototypes to validate the business concept.

2. Side Hustle Expansion:

• Objective: Grow the software development side hustle into a sustainable income stream.

• Strategies:

• Marketing: Increase online presence through targeted marketing efforts.

• Client Relationships: Cultivate strong relationships with existing clients for repeat business.

• Skill Enhancement: Stay updated on the latest programming languages and technologies.

3. Investment Portfolio Development:

• Objective: Build a diversified investment portfolio for long-term wealth growth.

• Strategies:

• Financial Literacy: Continuously educate oneself about investment opportunities.

• Risk Management: Balance high-risk, high-reward investments with more stable options.

• Professional Guidance: Seek advice from financial advisors for informed decision-making.

4. Real Estate Ventures:

• Objective: Acquire income-generating properties for long-term financial stability.

• Strategies:

• Research: Explore opportunities in the real estate market, including emerging areas.

• Financial Planning: Secure financing options and develop a strategic acquisition plan.

• Property Management: Implement efficient property management systems.

5. Scaling and Automation:

• Objective: Scale the tech startup operations and automate repetitive tasks.

• Strategies:

• Hiring: Recruit skilled professionals to support business expansion.

• Automation Tools: Implement technology to streamline operations.

• Efficiency Monitoring: Regularly assess processes for optimization opportunities.

Muhammed's Entrepreneurial Pursuit Plan

1. Eco-Friendly Business Growth:

• Objective: Expand the eco-friendly business and establish it as a sustainable brand.

• Strategies:

• Product Diversification: Introduce new eco-friendly products to cater to diverse markets.

• Market Expansion: Identify and enter new geographical markets.

• Brand Positioning: Emphasize the brand's commitment to sustainability in marketing.

2. Partnerships and Collaborations:

• Objective: Form strategic partnerships to enhance market reach and impact.

• Strategies:

• Networking: Attend industry events to connect with potential partners.

• Value Proposition: Clearly communicate the mutual benefits of collaboration.

• Joint Marketing: Collaborate on marketing initiatives to leverage shared audiences.

3. Investing in Renewable Energy:

• Objective: Invest in renewable energy projects aligning with sustainability goals.

• Strategies:

• Research: Identify viable renewable energy investment opportunities.

• Due Diligence: Conduct thorough analysis of potential projects.

• Long-Term Impact: Prioritize investments with positive environmental impacts.

4. Consulting and Workshops:

• Objective: Monetize sustainability expertise through consulting and workshops.

• Strategies:

• Online Presence: To draw in customers, have a powerful online presence.

• Knowledge Sharing: Develop informative workshops on sustainable practices.

• Client Education: Provide consulting services to businesses aiming to adopt eco-friendly practices.

5. Scaling and Automation:

• Objective: Scale product lines and automate processes for efficiency.

• Strategies:

• Supply Chain Optimization: Implement systems for streamlined product manufacturing.

• Automation Tools: Explore technologies to automate routine business tasks.

• Market Demand Analysis: Align scaling efforts with market demand.

6. Passive Income Streams:

• Objective: Generate passive income through investments and expertise.

• Strategies:

• Investment Portfolio: Build a diversified portfolio for long-term returns.

• Online Courses: Develop and market online courses on sustainability.

• Affiliate Marketing: Explore opportunities to earn through affiliate marketing related to sustainability.

7. Giving Back and Monetizing Passion:

• Objective: Integrate philanthropy into the business model and monetize passion projects.

• Strategies:

• Philanthropy Initiatives: Allocate a portion of profits to environmental causes.

• Educational Platforms: Create blogs and podcasts to share knowledge and generate additional income.

8. Exit Strategies and Portfolio Management:

• Objective: Plan for strategic exits and continually manage the business and investment portfolio.

• Strategies:

• Regular Assessments: Periodically evaluate the performance of business ventures.

• Strategic Exits: Consider selling successful ventures to fund new initiatives.

• Risk Mitigation: Diversify the business and investment portfolio to manage risks effectively.

These entrepreneurial pursuit plans outline the specific objectives, strategies, and actions that John and Muhammed will undertake to achieve their financial goals and build a diversified set of income streams. Their plans reflect a blend of innovation, strategic thinking, and a commitment to sustainability.

Monitoring and Adaptation:

1. Performance Metrics (Both):

• Key Performance Indicators (KPIs): Regularly track and analyze KPIs related to business performance, investment returns, and sustainability impact.

• Financial Reports: Generate detailed financial reports to assess the profitability and growth of each venture.

2. Adaptability (Both):

• Market Trends: Stay attuned to market trends, technological advancements, and shifts in consumer behavior.

• Feedback Mechanisms: Solicit and incorporate feedback from customers, mentors, and industry experts to adapt strategies.

COMMUNITY ENGAGEMENT:

1. Mentorship (Both):

• Entrepreneurial Community: Engage in mentorship programs to share experiences and insights with aspiring entrepreneurs.

• Networking Events: Attend and host networking events to foster connections within the entrepreneurial community.

2. Philanthropy (Both):

• Community Impact: Continue contributing to philanthropic initiatives, making a positive impact on local and global communities.

• Social Responsibility: Integrate socially responsible practices into business operations to enhance corporate social responsibility.

Future Planning

1. Innovation (Both):

• Continuous Innovation: Foster a culture of innovation within their businesses to stay ahead of the competition.

• Research and Development: Invest in research and development to explore new product/service offerings and business models.

2. Legacy Planning (Both):

• Succession Planning: Develop succession plans for the businesses to ensure continuity and legacy.

• Impact Beyond Finance: Consider the broader impact of their ventures on future generations and the environment.

Conclusion

As John and Muhammed embark on their entrepreneurial journeys, these plans provide a roadmap for achieving financial success, personal fulfillment, and positive societal impact. The outlined strategies are not rigid but flexible, allowing for adaptation to an ever-changing business landscape. By continually monitoring, adapting, engaging with the community, and planning for the future, John and Muhammed aim not only to attain their financial goals but to leave a lasting legacy built on innovation, sustainability, and a commitment to making a difference.

www.ingramcontent.com/pod-product-compliance
Lightning Source LLC
Chambersburg PA
CBHW060013300526
45794CB00003B/1182